JUDITH COSBY

Weaving Threads
of
Gratitude

JOURNAL

Weaving Threads of Gratitude, Journal

To protect the privacy of certain individuals, the names and identifying details have been changed.

This book is not intended to be a substitute for the medical or mental health advice of a licensed physician. The reader should consult with their doctor in any matters relating to his/her health.

Cover design and illustrations by Ana Grigoriu–Voicu, Books Design

ISBN-13: 978-1-7341153-2-1 (print book)

1. Time Management, 2. Mindfulness, 3. Gratitude, 4. Journaling, 5. Gifts, 6. Self Help, 7. Empowerment, 8. Personal Growth

First edition

Visit my website at www.judithcosby.com

"I don't have to chase extraordinary moments to find happiness – it's right in front of me if I'm paying attention and practicing gratitude."

~ Brene Brown

Begin your journey of reflection and learn how to cultivate your garden

Developing a consistent daily routine of capturing thankful moments and journaling them will encourage peace and happiness in your life. This life-changing journey will strengthen mindfulness and self-reflection and inspire empowerment. Expressing gratitude shows a level of thankfulness for what you have. This act, in turn, produces a level of kindness.

Meditating, finding a special space, lighting a candle, playing soft music, or sitting in prayer are all ways to encourage the positive thoughts of the day. Shutting out the noises and the constant barrage of exterior interruptions will help you value the time you have allotted for journaling. Performing these activities would be an excellent way to quiet the mind and recollect those special moments from the beginning/end of each day.

This cathartic journaling tool will visually show you the growth you experience through the clarity and mindfulness of the exercise of writing. By recording those positive events of the day, you will help retrain your thoughts from negative to positive. Cultivate your garden so that it grows and blooms into a life filled with gratitude and thankfulness.

WEEK 1

"There's just something beautiful about walking on snow that nobody else has walked on. It makes you believe you're special, even though you know you're not."

~ Carol Rifka Brunt

*T*he first time I ever witnessed a wild fox was in the morning after a heavy snowfall that had raged throughout the night. Leaving early in the morning for a walk with my husband and our two dogs, we began our trek on untouched snow. It was as if we had stepped inside a giant snow globe. The only sound we heard was the crunching of snow beneath our feet and paws. Although my sixth sense felt something watching me, it wasn't until I caught a glimpse of a beautiful rusty red coat in the distance that I felt this incredible connection. Her intense eyes, black stocking legs, and bushy tail called to me like nothing ever before. That meeting had a profound impact on my life. The stark red of her coat against the snow's pristine white made me feel as if I had experienced something extraordinary. Little did I know it was to be a harbinger of inspiration for the commencement of my new year.

Starting the day with a blank canvas of white enlivens us with limitless possibilities of what we want to accomplish. As we begin our journey into the days ahead, we hope to find new ideas and connections to help us on our way. Welcoming new souls, embracing humorous moments, and loving the ordinary times of our lives is a great way to add beauty to the next 365 days of the year.

Journal how you would like to see the next year of your life unfold. What goals or life changes do you hope to accomplish?

~ Threads of Reflection ~

Today I am grateful for: ♥
  Monday

_____
_____
_____
_____

Today I am grateful for: ♥
  Tuesday

_____
_____
_____
_____

Today I am grateful for: ♥
  Wednesday

_____
_____
_____
_____

Today I am grateful for:
   Thursday

_____
_____
_____
_____

Today I am grateful for:
   Friday

_____
_____
_____
_____

Today I am grateful for:
   Saturday

_____
_____
_____
_____

Today I am grateful for:
   Sunday

_____
_____
_____
_____

~Weaving Threads of Gratitude~

How do I cultivate my garden?

WEEK 2

"The heart of the man is very much like the sea, it has its storms, it has its tides and in its depths it has its pearls too."

~ Vincent Van Gogh

*T*his quote reminds me of the Christmas I received my first journal. I was 13 years old and found that gift to be inconsequential to the material presents I had received. But it was later that I discovered the journal had a magic to it. It called to me to write so many beautiful things within its blank pages. That book held my heart's desire: to become an author. After 35 years, I found it again in an old, dusty memorabilia box and began to re-read the life of a person I hardly knew anymore. Although self-doubt had emerged several times in my life to dissuade my dream to become an author, it was that little red journal that stood the test of time as a bright reminder to finish what I longed to accomplish.

It is so important to know that we all possess wonderful qualities and talents that can lead us to incredible places if only we have the courage and faith to believe in ourselves. Imagine that untapped potential within you as a beacon of beautiful light, which can be as simple as a white light or as elaborate as a rainbow. Shine that beautiful light out into the world, do not allow it to be extinguished.

Journal about the talents or gifts you possess and how you share them with others?

~ *Threads of Reflection* ~

Today I am grateful for:
  Monday

_____
_____
_____
_____

Today I am grateful for:
  Tuesday

_____
_____
_____
_____

Today I am grateful for:
  Wednesday

_____
_____
_____
_____

Today I am grateful for:
   Thursday

_____
_____
_____
_____

Today I am grateful for:
   Friday

_____
_____
_____
_____

Today I am grateful for:
   Saturday

_____
_____
_____
_____

Today I am grateful for:
   Sunday

_____
_____
_____
_____

~Weaving Threads of Gratitude~

How do I cultivate my garden?

WEEK 3

"Rest but never quit. Even a sun has a sinking spell each evening. But it always rises the next morning. At sunrise, every soul is born again."

~ Author Unknown

The song "Sunrise, Sunset" from Fiddler on the Roof, will forever remind me of the meaning of the sunrise and sunset of my own life. I chose that song for my father/daughter dance at my wedding. It was more poignant than I ever realized as I left the status of being my parent's little girl to becoming a married woman with a home of my own. The progression of each of my life stages since that day has brought about more profound respect in embracing the sunrises and sunsets of my life.

Sunrises and sunsets are the colors of our souls. They mark the beginning and end of each day. These moments remind us of the beauty of yesterday, the accomplishments of today, and the hope for tomorrow. They can also be used metaphorically as the expression of a beginning and end of a segment of life. Each sunrise begins with endless possibilities and finishes with the conclusion of that day's goals and dreams with hopes of meeting them again in the next morning.

Describe the goals and accomplishments that make your heart feel joy. Which ones are more significant in your daily life? Are there some that are harder to obtain? Why?

~ Threads of Reflection ~

Today I am grateful for:
Monday

Today I am grateful for:
Tuesday

Today I am grateful for:
Wednesday

Today I am grateful for:
  Thursday

_____
_____
_____
_____

Today I am grateful for:
  Friday

_____
_____
_____
_____

Today I am grateful for:
  Saturday

_____
_____
_____
_____

Today I am grateful for:
  Sunday

_____
_____
_____
_____

~Weaving Threads of Gratitude~

How do I cultivate my garden?

WEEK 4

"A single act of kindness throws out roots in all directions, and the roots spring up and make new trees. The greatest work that kindness does to others is that it makes them kind themselves."

~ Amelia Earhart

Some people bring a positive vibe and energy to everything they touch. I know several of them personally, and their gifts of goodness abound with everything they do. They breathe life into the events they attend, encourage community service through good works, and recognize when friends and neighbors need assistance. They do these good works without any requirement of payment or expectation of return. I have benefited personally from these kind people, and they have inspired me to continue to pay it forward wherever and whenever I can.

Goodness and kindness walk hand in hand with the ethics and morals we carry within each of us. Paying it forward, creating goodwill, and all acts of kindness create a beautiful light that makes the world a brighter place. Practicing one kind act a day, no matter how small, makes a difference not only in your life but in the lives of others.

Journal the kindness you received and how you chose to share your goodness with those around you.

~ Threads of Reflection ~

Today I am grateful for: 🖤
Monday

_____
_____
_____
_____

Today I am grateful for: 🖤
Tuesday

_____
_____
_____
_____

Today I am grateful for: 🖤
Wednesday

_____
_____
_____
_____

Today I am grateful for:
  Thursday

Today I am grateful for:
  Friday

Today I am grateful for:
  Saturday

Today I am grateful for:
  Sunday

~Weaving Threads of Gratitude~

How do I cultivate my garden?

WEEK 5

"It's not about getting by. It's about the stack of tiny little moments of joy and love that add up to a lifetime that's been worthwhile. You can't measure them; you can only capture them; like snapshots in your mind."

~ C. Robert Cargill

While recalling a trip my eldest daughter had taken to Arizona, I was struck by the memory that came to mind. Embarking on her first solo vacation, my mother had offered to accompany us on the ride to the airport. There we were, three generations, laughing and talking as we drove. Each of us reveling in my daughter's independence and sharing our love for one another. Such a beautiful picture stored within the confines of my mind.

There will be times when we are unaware of the importance of the moments being woven into our tapestries. By living your life with the understanding that although a given moment may seem insignificant, it may later shine with a flash of brilliance, you never noticed before. It is not the monumental moments that will impact your life, but rather the ones that are ordinary in design.

Try to recall moments that have a greater significance to them than what you originally had thought. Journal those experiences and what you have learned from them.

~ Threads of Reflection ~

Today I am grateful for:
  Monday

_____

Today I am grateful for:
  Tuesday

_____

Today I am grateful for:
  Wednesday

_____

Today I am grateful for:
  Thursday

_____
_____
_____
_____

Today I am grateful for:
  Friday

_____
_____
_____
_____

Today I am grateful for:
  Saturday

_____
_____
_____
_____

Today I am grateful for:
  Sunday

_____
_____
_____
_____

~Weaving Threads of Gratitude~

How do I cultivate my garden?

WEEK 6

"It is by fighting the limitations, temptations, and failures of the world that we reach our highest possibilities."

~ Helen Keller

*U*pon receiving the initial diagnosis of my youngest daughter's illness and facing the unknown, I felt almost sucker-punched by the magnitude of its gravity. But as the days passed and treatments began to unfold before us, we were awestruck by the amazing people who joined our road and walked with us. The acceptance of the disease, the strength it took to battle, and the unity we felt to fight this side by side were life-changing. I do believe that it was a turning point for my entire family, and we are closer because of it. We have learned so much about ourselves and what we truly desire. A beautiful blessing of ordinary days.

When life hits you with an unexpected turn and the thought of dealing with pitfalls beyond your control is too much to bear, then you must dig deep within yourself to find a way to overcome these difficulties. Hope is key to surviving these challenges, and with hope comes the strength and courage needed to triumph over this turmoil. Believe that you can, and you will. Overcoming and acceptance go hand in hand in making a better version of ourselves.

Journal how you feel when acceptance of a challenge is inevitable. Reflect on ways you can triumph over adversity and challenging times. Identify the coping mechanisms used during those moments.

~ *Threads of Reflection* ~

Today I am grateful for:
  Monday

_____
_____
_____
_____

Today I am grateful for:
  Tuesday

_____
_____
_____
_____

Today I am grateful for:
  Wednesday

_____
_____
_____
_____

Today I am grateful for:
   Thursday

_____
_____
_____
_____

Today I am grateful for:
   Friday

_____
_____
_____
_____

Today I am grateful for:
   Saturday

_____
_____
_____
_____

Today I am grateful for:
   Sunday

_____
_____
_____
_____

~Weaving Threads of Gratitude~

How do I cultivate my garden?

WEEK 7

"Those who enter the gates of heaven are not beings who have no passions or who have curbed passions, but those who have cultivated an understanding of them."

~ William Blake

When my neighborhood was faced with a decision at a town meeting to have speed humps placed on our streets, many neighbors came with opposing views. As the discussions increased regarding the decision, passions arose. Neighbors who were usually very pleasant and civil became tense as each side presented their case. The conversation, in general, became heated, and I became acutely aware of the emotion growing within me. The ability to temper my reactions and see the value in the relationship with my neighbors helped quell the impending disagreement. When the meeting was over, I was able to walk outside and chat in a friendly way with my neighbors. Cultivating my emotion allowed me to retain my relationships.

Emotions can cloud our judgment and, when engaged in an argument, can often leave us with regret. Passion brings our tapestries to life with a vibrancy of colors and movement. Adverse reactions can be very destructive to our picture if not handled appropriately. Learning to temper our emotions allows us to weave a more positive version of ourselves.

Can you find ways in which you were able to curb your anger or diffuse difficult situations? Try to reset your clock to zero and see how you can go forward with ways to temper your reactions into a more positive outcome.

~ *Threads of Reflection* ~

Today I am grateful for:
  Monday

_____
_____
_____
_____

Today I am grateful for:
  Tuesday

_____
_____
_____
_____

Today I am grateful for:
  Wednesday

_____
_____
_____
_____

Today I am grateful for:
  Thursday

_____
_____
_____
_____

Today I am grateful for:
  Friday

_____
_____
_____
_____

Today I am grateful for:
  Saturday

_____
_____
_____
_____

Today I am grateful for:
  Sunday

_____
_____
_____
_____

~Weaving Threads of Gratitude~

How do I cultivate my garden?

WEEK 8

"I believe in the old, because it shows us where we come from – where our souls have risen from. And I believe in the new, because it gives us the opportunity to create who we are becoming."

~ Abigail Washburn

I have a family member who was adopted and raised by a loving set of parents. Although she never knew her birth parents, she could not help but wonder if their specific physiological and psychological traits defined her. Her ties to them ended the day she was born, and everything she became was through the loving family that raised her. The only thing she knew was that she was eternally grateful for her life and chose to do beautiful things with it. I, too, was so very thankful she was born because she had a profound impact on my early life and continues to do so to this very day.

Despite the origin of where we began, we have infinite opportunities to become a better version of ourselves. Never stop trying to make a more positive impact on the world around you. Loving yourself, striving for excellence, and sharing your gifts with others are all wonderful ways to become what you envision.

Journal how you inspire others. In what ways do you strive to become the best version of yourself?

~ *Threads of Reflection* ~

Today I am grateful for:
  Monday

_____
_____
_____
_____

Today I am grateful for:
  Tuesday

_____
_____
_____
_____

Today I am grateful for:
  Wednesday

_____
_____
_____
_____

Today I am grateful for: 🖤
  Thursday

_____
_____
_____
_____

Today I am grateful for: 🖤
  Friday

_____
_____
_____
_____

Today I am grateful for: 🖤
  Saturday

_____
_____
_____
_____

Today I am grateful for: 🖤
  Sunday

_____
_____
_____
_____

~Weaving Threads of Gratitude~

How do I cultivate my garden?

WEEK 9

"The hardest thing to ever do is to reveal the naked soul to the world. However, in doing so brings healing, growth, strength, and powerful inspiration!"

~ H.E. Olsen

*P*hysical and emotional pain can be draining. The experience of family alienation was one of the most profound and painful moments of my life. Once I acknowledged how I felt and was able to forgive, I could then heal and move forward in my own life. Revealing that hurt openly and releasing it out into the world gave me the strength to no longer hold it inside to fester. Within that revelation came the ability to mend and grow positively.

We must be courageous and open to welcoming pain within our lives. Although there is a natural aversion to it, facing emotional pain allows us to avoid reliving a negative experience again. Re-examining negative life experiences enables us to bring forth something positive from past struggles and, in doing so, makes us whole again.

Journal moments where you felt overwhelmed and saddened by an event. Re-read it and identify what was painful about the experience and how you could learn and grow from it.

~ Threads of Reflection ~

Today I am grateful for:
  Monday

_____
_____
_____
_____

Today I am grateful for:
  Tuesday

_____
_____
_____
_____

Today I am grateful for:
  Wednesday

_____
_____
_____
_____

Today I am grateful for:
  Thursday

_____
_____
_____
_____

Today I am grateful for:
  Friday

_____
_____
_____
_____

Today I am grateful for:
  Saturday

_____
_____
_____
_____

Today I am grateful for:
  Sunday

_____
_____
_____
_____

~Weaving Threads of Gratitude~

How do I cultivate my garden?

WEEK 10

"Dare to love yourself as if you were a rainbow with gold at both ends."

~ Aberjhani

*I*t is hard to invest in ourselves when life pulls us in all directions. During a time when I needed inspiration and quiet, I decided to go on a long weekend writer's retreat in a remote part of Vermont. Although I was there to perfect my craft of writing, I soon discovered that it also tempered my soul. In that beautiful mountain retreat setting, only the sounds of nature were heard. As I sat by a large pond writing, I became acutely aware of the bees buzzing, the sound of the wind over the cattails and reeds, the flutter of hummingbirds flitting about, and the ordinary silence that comes from being one with nature. After I returned home, I felt so invigorated and peaceful.

We have the tendency not to allow ourselves the time and the space to heal our bodies, minds, and souls completely, but rather expend all of our energies on the outer world. But if we were to treat ourselves with a timeframe that encouraged simplicity and healing, we would enhance our lives with a fresher and sharper image. It is essential to our health that we allow the time to be kind to ourselves. Walking, meditating, yoga, or other introspective activities relieve our stress and invite the respite needed to regroup our inner peace. Invest in your well-being and take notice of the different ways you were able to soothe your soul and invigorate your body.

Record the activities that bring a sense of calm and self-reflection into your life. Return to this section often as a reminder.

~ Threads of Reflection ~

Today I am grateful for: ♥
   Monday

_____
_____
_____
_____

Today I am grateful for: ♥
   Tuesday

_____
_____
_____
_____

Today I am grateful for: ♥
   Wednesday

_____
_____
_____
_____

Today I am grateful for:
  Thursday

_____
_____
_____
_____

Today I am grateful for:
  Friday

_____
_____
_____
_____

Today I am grateful for:
  Saturday

_____
_____
_____
_____

Today I am grateful for:
  Sunday

_____
_____
_____
_____

~Weaving Threads of Gratitude~

How do I cultivate my garden?

WEEK 11

"I don't know whether you can look at your past and find, woven like the hidden symbols on a treasure map, the path that will point to your final destination."

~ Jodi Picoult

I have been very fortunate to have incredible people in my life. One person, in particular, had a profound impact on me. We first met when we had graduated from college and began our careers together, full of youth and exuberance. We separated for a time, leading our lives in different directions, only to rejoin at a later point when we were both faced with the severe illness of a child. Each of us became a support system to one another as we walked a similar road, tethering our tapestries together with encouragement and love.

Each one of us has a destiny and a direction unique to our creation. We follow these paths at our own pace and time. The roads differ in many ways. Some are surefooted and short, and some are long and uncertain. Some roads lead us to destinations we did not even imagine. We also have the opportunity to walk these roads with other travelers. Some connections will be short, some long, and some separate and rejoin at a later date. These people are placed on our paths, not by accident, but as companions to support us on our life's journey.

Journal about those people who touched you deeply and brought about positivity and goodness to your life. Have they been a constant in your life? What made their connection so special?

~ Threads of Reflection ~

Today I am grateful for: 🩶
Monday

_____
_____
_____
_____

Today I am grateful for: 🩶
Tuesday

_____
_____
_____
_____

Today I am grateful for: 🩶
Wednesday

_____
_____
_____
_____

Today I am grateful for:
  Thursday

_____
_____
_____
_____

Today I am grateful for:
  Friday

_____
_____
_____
_____

Today I am grateful for:
  Saturday

_____
_____
_____
_____

Today I am grateful for:
  Sunday

_____
_____
_____
_____

~Weaving Threads of Gratitude~

How do I cultivate my garden?

WEEK 12

"Like a welcome summer rain, humor may suddenly cleanse and cool the earth, the air, and you."

~ Langston Hughes

Some of the funniest moments in my life have stemmed from my most embarrassing situations. What I have learned from those moments is that I can genuinely laugh at myself. Once, while working out at the gym on an elliptical trainer, I was feeling good about myself. I was moving along, bopping to the music in my headphones and loving the new workout outfit that I had just purchased. Glancing around, I happened to catch a glimpse of myself in the floor-to-ceiling mirrored wall. To my horror, my new workout shirt was on backward and inside out! I wasn't ready to stop my work out but suddenly became acutely aware of my predicament. Instead, I just kept on going and laughed about it with anyone I could. It ended up making the workout so much fun.

Humor is a gift that should be enjoyed daily. Without this gift in our lives, the weaves of our tapestries would become knotted and tight, and the colors would not be allowed to dance freely within its body and seams. It lightens the soul and brings joyous energy to our life.

Try to incorporate humor within your life and watch how the darkest of times become lighter, full of hope, and positive. Journal the humorous things that brought laughter to your life.

~ Threads of Reflection ~

Today I am grateful for:
Monday

_____
_____
_____
_____

Today I am grateful for:
Tuesday

_____
_____
_____
_____

Today I am grateful for:
Wednesday

_____
_____
_____
_____

Today I am grateful for:
  Thursday

Today I am grateful for:
  Friday

Today I am grateful for:
  Saturday

Today I am grateful for:
  Sunday

~Weaving Threads of Gratitude~

How do I cultivate my garden?

WEEK 13

"When you photograph people in color, you photograph their clothes. But when you photograph people in black and white, your photograph their souls."

~ Ted Grant

*W*hen faced with dark moments in my life, I am always amazed at the light sent my way to help guide me through those difficult times. I recall a moment when a family friend stopped by after work to drop off some polished stones and acrylic paint. My daughter had just been released from her third hospitalization in less than five months. We were tired and overwhelmed. My friend came by like a beacon of light to share her gift of painting mandala stones. It was a gift of pure goodness, and the quality of time we spent creating the designs was therapeutic and a calming light to our souls.

Significant moments of black and white are interwoven within our tapestries. Within the darkness that can encompass our lives at any given time, there is also the glint of white light that brings forth hope and promise for a better experience. Gratefulness emerges when we see the positive through the negative.

Journal how you have recognized beacons of light in the forms of people during difficult times. How did they help you?

~ *Threads of Reflection* ~

Today I am grateful for:
   Monday

_____
_____
_____
_____

Today I am grateful for:
   Tuesday

_____
_____
_____
_____

Today I am grateful for:
   Wednesday

_____
_____
_____
_____

Today I am grateful for:
   Thursday

_____
_____
_____
_____

Today I am grateful for:
   Friday

_____
_____
_____
_____

Today I am grateful for:
   Saturday

_____
_____
_____
_____

Today I am grateful for:
   Sunday

_____
_____
_____
_____

~Weaving Threads of Gratitude~

How do I cultivate my garden?

WEEK 14

"Stir the world with your skills, shake the world with your talents, move the world with your brilliance, change the world with your genius."

~ Matshona Dhliwayo

I have a genuine love for animals. To my family, I am nicknamed "Doolittle," to others I am known as "the animal whisperer." I come by it naturally, with very little fear and an all-knowing of what the animals are feeling and saying with their eyes. I have been a part of many animal rescues throughout my life; turtles, baby bunnies, wild birds, cats, and dogs. Even though I can't save every suffering animal in this world, I feel that my small donations of time and treasure make a difference. I may be just a tiny ripple in the ocean, but I make a difference in saving the lives of animals. My gift is modest, but I plan to use it every time I am called to action.

The gifts we offer the world don't have to be significant or newsworthy, but they should be recognized and utilized. We come at life with an array of gifts; spiritual, technical, creative, and athletic. Find your gift and share it to make the world a better place.

Journal the gift(s) that you possess and how you will continue to make those blessings available to others.

~ *Threads of Reflection* ~

Today I am grateful for: ♥
  Monday

_____
_____
_____
_____

Today I am grateful for: ♥
  Tuesday

_____
_____
_____
_____

Today I am grateful for: ♥
  Wednesday

_____
_____
_____
_____

Today I am grateful for:
  Thursday

_____
_____
_____
_____

Today I am grateful for:
  Friday

_____
_____
_____
_____

Today I am grateful for:
  Saturday

_____
_____
_____
_____

Today I am grateful for:
  Sunday

_____
_____
_____
_____

~Weaving Threads of Gratitude~

How do I cultivate my garden?

WEEK 15

"Begin doing what you want to do now. We are not living in eternity. We have only this moment, sparkling like a star in our hand-and melting like a snowflake."

~ Sir Francis Bacon

While strolling along Easton's Beach in Newport, Rhode Island, one sunny Sunday morning, I watched the other walkers talking to one another and embracing that beautiful day. Groups of seagulls ran in and out of the water as dogs ran about the shoreline chasing invisible prey. The sun had created a mirror reflection in the veil of seafoam and wet sand beneath it. I became acutely aware of all of the beauty of this shoreline paradise and the calm and serenity it presented. This mindfulness added a depth and richness to my tapestry.

Mindfulness is key to recognizing the things that surround us. Awareness does not require a grandness of moment or vibrancy of exchange, but rather an openness to see all of the beautiful things that encompass our lives. Have you ever taken note of a spectacular blue sky, a mesmerizing full moon, or an awe-inspiring mountain top? Those visuals can invigorate the senses and inspire us. Simple images can be just as inspiring, such as an elegant butterfly atop a beautiful flower. Sometimes the most wonderful things to take notice of are the smallest and ordinary parts of our day.

Record your mindfulness journey as you see the world around you with fresh new eyes. Continue to keep close attention to all of the things, big and small, that enliven your life.

~ Threads of Reflection ~

Today I am grateful for: 💜
  Monday

_____
_____
_____
_____

Today I am grateful for: 💜
  Tuesday

_____
_____
_____
_____

Today I am grateful for: 💜
  Wednesday

_____
_____
_____
_____

Today I am grateful for:
Thursday

_____
_____
_____
_____

Today I am grateful for:
Friday

_____
_____
_____
_____

Today I am grateful for:
Saturday

_____
_____
_____
_____

Today I am grateful for:
Sunday

_____
_____
_____
_____

~Weaving Threads of Gratitude~

How do I cultivate my garden?

WEEK 16

"I don't want a rainbow… Rainbows have too many colors and none of them receive the appreciation they deserve… I'd prefer a fading red or a striking golden, a shimmery silver or a sober blue… Ruling the sunset sky alone!"

~ Debalina Haldar

*W*alking amongst my gardens, I am always intrigued by the variety of colors and scents that arise from them. My water garden is a plethora of colors that seem to reflect within the swirling water, creating a kaleidoscope image. My perennial garden is a symphony of pinks, reds, and purples in all different shapes and sizes. The hydrangeas that flank the edges of my home bring an array of color variations within its cluster of blooms. I love the broad spectrum of color seen from afar. Still, my favorite part of my gardens is my morning walkthrough, examining each color and shape individually and marveling at its beauty.

Weaving the colors of our lives into a multitude of hues or appreciating them one by one is what makes our spirit burst forth with gratitude and joy. Rainbows bring forth feelings of hope and promise. Embracing their distinctive colors brings about clarity.

Journal what experiencing the five senses mean to you and how they bring clarity to your life. Which ones inspire you?

~ Threads of Reflection ~

Today I am grateful for: 🖤
  Monday

_____

_____

_____

_____

Today I am grateful for: 🖤
  Tuesday

_____

_____

_____

_____

Today I am grateful for: 🖤
  Wednesday

_____

_____

_____

_____

Today I am grateful for:
  Thursday

_____
_____
_____
_____

Today I am grateful for:
  Friday

_____
_____
_____
_____

Today I am grateful for:
  Saturday

_____
_____
_____
_____

Today I am grateful for:
  Sunday

_____
_____
_____
_____

~Weaving Threads of Gratitude~

How do I cultivate my garden?

WEEK 17

"An invisible red thread connects those who are destined to meet, regardless of time, place, or circumstance. The thread may stretch or tangle, but will never break."

~ Ancient Chinese Proverb

I truly believe we meet people on our paths that lead us in directions we are meant to follow. They arrive at precisely the right moment, redirecting us towards our intended goals. Many years ago, I took a massive leap of faith and joined a writer's retreat in the mountains of Vermont. It was not only life-changing, but the author I connected with was instrumental in helping me pursue my goal. After the retreat had ended, she continued to be an invaluable mentor to my writing journey. I believe we met each other to become an incredible support system for one another.

There are people in our lives that we are destined to meet. Regardless of the circumstances, there is a pre-designed and perfect path for those meant to be in our lives. Embracing this idea and treasuring those connections is the highest form of gratefulness we could practice every day.

Journal about the people in your life and why you are grateful for their presence in it. What unique circumstances brought you together?

~ *Threads of Reflection* ~

Today I am grateful for: 🖤
   Monday

_____
_____
_____
_____

Today I am grateful for: 🖤
   Tuesday

_____
_____
_____
_____

Today I am grateful for: 🖤
   Wednesday

_____
_____
_____
_____

Today I am grateful for:
  Thursday

_____
_____
_____
_____

Today I am grateful for:
  Friday

_____
_____
_____
_____

Today I am grateful for:
  Saturday

_____
_____
_____
_____

Today I am grateful for:
  Sunday

_____
_____
_____
_____

~Weaving Threads of Gratitude~

How do I cultivate my garden?

WEEK 18

"Sometimes you have to let go of the picture of what you thought life would be like and learn to find joy in the story you are actually living."

~ Rachel Marie Martin

I have always believed I had experienced a level of grace when I first read this quote. I came across it during a visit to Dana Farber in Boston during a challenging time with the serious illness of my youngest daughter. I never expected to be faced with any level of hardship or illness with either one of my daughters. But during a tumultuous time, I was forced to accept this challenge and face it head-on with fortitude and faith. By accepting this trial, a level of grace emerged, and a fight to embrace every day with a hopeful and positive mantra helped get us through. Sometimes we have to let go of the life we had pictured for ourselves and those we love and begin embracing the joy of the life we were given.

Even in difficult times, we need to find enjoyment in the journey. It may require some digging down deep to discover that place where we can find solace and peace within our lives. Counting the blessings that are bestowed upon us and working on those positives can shed light on all of the beautiful gifts that surround us.

Journal how you were able to accept the challenges given and how you found happiness within those gems of reality.

~ *Threads of Reflection* ~

Today I am grateful for:
  Monday

_____
_____
_____
_____

Today I am grateful for:
  Tuesday

_____
_____
_____
_____

Today I am grateful for:
  Wednesday

_____
_____
_____
_____

Today I am grateful for: 💜
  Thursday

_____
_____
_____
_____

Today I am grateful for: 💜
  Friday

_____
_____
_____
_____

Today I am grateful for: 💜
  Saturday

_____
_____
_____
_____

Today I am grateful for: 💜
  Sunday

_____
_____
_____
_____

~Weaving Threads of Gratitude~

How do I cultivate my garden?

WEEK 19

Brushing the clouds away from my eyes, I see clarity in the raindrop and beauty in the first ray of morning sun… Life is strange and wondrous."

~ Virginia Alison

*W*alking along the seaside and taking in the sights is so calming. I have my favorite spots along the Cliff Walk in Newport, Rhode Island, where I like just to sit and listen. I love to hear the sounds of the ocean hitting against the massive rocks that line this stretch of land. The constant ebb and flow of its movement lull me into a trance. The seagulls make their sharp squawking call within the salty air, beckoning me to look up into the sky and find them. My breathing becomes softer, my mind becomes clearer, and my heart becomes fuller. Those are the times I feel closest to my core self.

Mindfulness allows us to look within ourselves without interpretation or judgement. During these instances of reflection, we get a glimpse into ourselves, warts, and all, and find gratitude for our life's blessings. We can achieve this level of mindfulness through occasions of calm, reflection, and acceptance of who we are—clarity at its finest.

Think of ways you can clear your mind and become one with all that surrounds you. What brings you peace of mind and heart?

~ Threads of Reflection ~

Today I am grateful for: 🩶
  Monday

_____
_____
_____
_____

Today I am grateful for: 🩶
  Tuesday

_____
_____
_____
_____

Today I am grateful for: 🩶
  Wednesday

_____
_____
_____
_____

Today I am grateful for:
  Thursday

_____
_____
_____
_____

Today I am grateful for:
  Friday

_____
_____
_____
_____

Today I am grateful for:
  Saturday

_____
_____
_____
_____

Today I am grateful for:
  Sunday

_____
_____
_____
_____

~Weaving Threads of Gratitude~

How do I cultivate my garden?

WEEK 20

"I love how summer just wraps its arms around you like a warm blanket."

~ Kellie Elmore

*W*alks on the beach in the early evening are very soulful moments. The throngs of crowds have gone, and the sun seems to cast a beautiful pink-orange glow on the horizon. How I love to walk the shore at night, feeling the cool evening breeze against my face, and listening to the constant roll of the waves as they kiss the shore. Those are the times I feel wrapped within the arms of summer, letting not just my body, but my entire being, sense its warmth and comfort, like a favorite blanket.

The peaceful days of summer encourage reflective moments, where we are just as happy being within our own skin, relishing all that we have in our immediate world and recognizing that being average and enjoying a simple existence can be magical. Summer weaves celebrate those times in our lives when we can kick back and enjoy the nature that surrounds us.

Journal the way summer makes you feel. Describe in that entry what specifically instills calm and tranquility within that reflection.

~ *Threads of Reflection* ~

Today I am grateful for:
  Monday

_____
_____
_____
_____

Today I am grateful for:
  Tuesday

_____
_____
_____
_____

Today I am grateful for:
  Wednesday

_____
_____
_____
_____

Today I am grateful for:
  Thursday

_____
_____
_____
_____

Today I am grateful for:
  Friday

_____
_____
_____
_____

Today I am grateful for:
  Saturday

_____
_____
_____
_____

Today I am grateful for:
  Sunday

_____
_____
_____
_____

~Weaving Threads of Gratitude~

How do I cultivate my garden?

WEEK 21

"To speak gratitude is courteous and pleasant, to enact gratitude is generous and noble, but to live gratitude is to touch heaven."

~ Johannes A. Gaertner

---

*O*ne day, I was sitting with an elderly family member. His eyes were not as sharp as they were in his youth, and his demeanor had softened through the years. A boisterous man with a booming voice, he had now become very gentle and mellow. He saw a dandelion in the lawn, bright yellow, and fully bloomed. Asking me to look closer at the dandelion, he shared how spectacular and perfectly formed it was. I, who initially thought the dandelion was the nemesis of every pristine lawn, now saw the beauty in its design. He shared his gratefulness for it and its uses, and I, too, suddenly felt thankful for the perfection of that beautiful little weed.

Gratefulness comes from a place of grace. Greet each day with a thankful heart for the blessings that abound. The regular habit of thankfulness is not as easy to achieve as it sounds and requires a significant amount of practice and patience. There will be days that will challenge you with negative occurrences. Weaving the colors and simple textures of gratitude allows us to temper our negative feelings and start the day on a foundation of good.

Journal all of the different ways that you feel joy and thankfulness. Were there specific occasions that inspired your gratitude?

~Threads of Reflection~

Today I am grateful for: ♥
  Monday

_____
_____
_____
_____

Today I am grateful for: ♥
  Tuesday

_____
_____
_____
_____

Today I am grateful for: ♥
  Wednesday

_____
_____
_____
_____

Today I am grateful for: 💜
  Thursday

_____
_____
_____
_____

Today I am grateful for: 💜
  Friday

_____
_____
_____
_____

Today I am grateful for: 💜
  Saturday

_____
_____
_____
_____

Today I am grateful for: 💜
  Sunday

_____
_____
_____
_____

~Weaving Threads of Gratitude~

How do I cultivate my garden?

WEEK 22

"Life, now, was unfolding before me, constantly and visibly, like the flowers of summer that drop fanlike petals on eternal soil."

~ Roman Payne

Self-reflection is a wonderful and soulful way to look at life. There were so many beautiful summer nights where I would sit outside on my deck and journal beside my koi pond. Listening to the waterfall splash, the lone calls of the birds as they settled in for the evening, and the chorus of the Katydids as they played their night song, ushered me into moments of thought and reflection. Clearing my mind and allowing the moments of the day to be written for examination gave me a sense of clarity and purpose.

By examining all of the moments that we weave into our days, weeks, and years, we allow ourselves a more profound and more wondrous opportunity to see what we have overcome, where we are going, and how incredible we are.

During moments of self-reflection, how did you see yourself? Did you remain true to your values and principals? Would you have done something differently?

~ *Threads of Reflection* ~

Today I am grateful for:
  Monday

_____

_____

_____

_____

Today I am grateful for:
  Tuesday

_____

_____

_____

_____

Today I am grateful for:
  Wednesday

_____

_____

_____

_____

Today I am grateful for:
  Thursday

_____
_____
_____
_____

Today I am grateful for:
  Friday

_____
_____
_____
_____

Today I am grateful for:
  Saturday

_____
_____
_____
_____

Today I am grateful for:
  Sunday

_____
_____
_____
_____

~Weaving Threads of Gratitude~

How do I cultivate my garden?

WEEK 23

"Invisible threads are the strongest ties."

~ Friedrich Nietzsche

*M*y Nana and I always had a close relationship. Our connection held a deep and invisible thread that bound us together from the moment our eyes met. She had a way of making me feel safe and loved, and our times together were extraordinary. Her faith in God was paramount, and she instilled that spiritual belief in me. My favorite thing about her was her infectious laugh. I loved to watch her cook her famous Portuguese dishes with her magical hands. She could make everything taste so delicious. She did not have much to give us, but her gift of food was her greatest joy. Those memories of her kitchen still bring a smile to my face. She is a beloved thread in my tapestry, and we are tethered together through eternity.

Those people we hold dearest to our hearts are the connections that weave in and out of our tapestry in the most significant ways. They give us a chance to learn from them and to become a better version of ourselves. These invisible threads tether us to those we love the most, and no matter how far apart we may become, that tie of love will always bind us together. Embracing these connections and using them as guideposts in our lives can point us to endless possibilities.

Think of all those who have positively impacted your life. Who would you consider to be a beloved thread in your tapestry?

~ *Threads of Reflection* ~

Today I am grateful for:
  Monday

_____
_____
_____
_____

Today I am grateful for:
  Tuesday

_____
_____
_____
_____

Today I am grateful for:
  Wednesday

_____
_____
_____
_____

Today I am grateful for:
  Thursday

_____
_____
_____
_____

Today I am grateful for:
  Friday

_____
_____
_____
_____

Today I am grateful for:
  Saturday

_____
_____
_____
_____

Today I am grateful for:
  Sunday

_____
_____
_____
_____

~Weaving Threads of Gratitude~

How do I cultivate my garden?

WEEK 24

"Summer has filled her veins with light and her heart is washed with noon."

~ C. Day-Lewis

*S*o many times, I have strolled our State Park and roamed the woods on dirt paths listening to the swooshing of the pine trees that grow so tall there. My dogs run along the river's edge playing within its moving water. This peaceful mecca of tranquility warms and enlivens me. Nature surrounds me with its sounds of buzzing bees and the melodic rustle of the leaves in the trees. These are the days of summer that bring contentment to my mind, body, and soul.

Experiencing mindfulness in the warmth of the sun brings about a serenity and calm to our lives. Listening to the chirping of the birds, the sounds of the waves crashing into the shore or the lapping water along a river's edge enlivens our senses. It encourages thankfulness and gratitude for what our world bestows upon us.

Write about the sounds and sights that encourage calm and peace in you. Identify the parts of nature that can bring namaste to your soul.

~ Threads of Reflection ~

Today I am grateful for:
Monday

_____
_____
_____
_____

Today I am grateful for:
Tuesday

_____
_____
_____
_____

Today I am grateful for:
Wednesday

_____
_____
_____
_____

Today I am grateful for:
  Thursday

_____
_____
_____
_____

Today I am grateful for:
  Friday

_____
_____
_____
_____

Today I am grateful for:
  Saturday

_____
_____
_____
_____

Today I am grateful for:
  Sunday

_____
_____
_____
_____

~Weaving Threads of Gratitude~

How do I cultivate my garden?

WEEK 25

"The summer weave has inspired me to spend these days with cheerfulness and liveliness. Embracing all of it with an exuberance that filled my being with exhilaration and a zest for life and things like vacation, fun summer activities, or outdoor family events."

~ Judith Cosby

My favorite activity in the summer is to run. As the years go by, my runs are much slower and no longer timed. But the joy of running along my favorite beach brings me a sense of peace and contentment that I rarely find anywhere else. It is my happy place. One day on the run along the shoreline, I found a dollar bill covered in sand, its tip waving in the wind. I knelt and grabbed it. This stretch of sand and shore was so precious to my spirit, I took the dollar bill and placed it in my sneaker and continued to finish my run. That dollar bill, now set within my gratitude jar, serves as a constant reminder that the greatest treasure for me is the time spent on my beautiful beach.

Experiencing these beautiful summertime moments that sparkle with a different shine brings about a deeper understanding of our inner being. Demonstrating moments of thankfulness brings about a clearer vision of our life's gifts and the treasures we hold closest to our hearts.

Journal the places that bring your heart the most happiness and gratitude. What items do you hold as a reminder of them?

~ *Threads of Reflection* ~

Today I am grateful for:
  Monday

_____
_____
_____
_____

Today I am grateful for:
  Tuesday

_____
_____
_____
_____

Today I am grateful for:
  Wednesday

_____
_____
_____
_____

Today I am grateful for:
   Thursday

_____
_____
_____
_____

Today I am grateful for:
   Friday

_____
_____
_____
_____

Today I am grateful for:
   Saturday

_____
_____
_____
_____

Today I am grateful for:
   Sunday

_____
_____
_____
_____

~Weaving Threads of Gratitude~

How do I cultivate my garden?

WEEK 26

"It's impossible," said pride. "It's risky," said experience. "It's pointless," said reason. "Give it a try," whispered the heart."

~ Author unknown

I confess I am an "inside the box" kind of person. I like routine and knowing what to expect. I try to be adventurous, but my practical inner voice will usually try to talk me out of it. Choosing to rescue and adopt another dog seemed almost insane at the time, but something was nagging at my heart. I felt compelled in a way I can't rationally describe, but listening to my heart and following my gut brought my family and me on the most incredible journey. Our home is filled with such joy since we adopted our "big guy." He is loved every day, and our family is complete with him in our lives.

Sometimes we need to listen to our inner voice and follow our hearts. Performing a good deed, experiencing a chance meeting, or choosing a new path are all wonderful ways to embrace the day. Have faith, and listen to your heart.

Journal about the opportunities that have arisen in your life and how you responded to them. Did those challenges inspire you to make a difference for others?

~ *Threads of Reflection* ~

Today I am grateful for:
   Monday

_____
_____
_____
_____

Today I am grateful for:
   Tuesday

_____
_____
_____
_____

Today I am grateful for:
   Wednesday

_____
_____
_____
_____

Today I am grateful for:
  Thursday

_____

Today I am grateful for:
  Friday

_____

Today I am grateful for:
  Saturday

_____

Today I am grateful for:
  Sunday

_____

~Weaving Threads of Gratitude~

How do I cultivate my garden?

WEEK 27

"On that magical day, the sun, sand, and sea transcended their individual reality and combined to bestow a peace upon all those who were present to witness it. Just being in that space and time had given each of us a chance to feel healthy, happy, and at complete ease with life."

~ Judith Cosby

*T*here were so many times when I walked upon my beloved beach in Rhode Island that I would feel as if I was walking on hallowed ground. Everything about that shoreline brought about an ambiance of peace to my soul. It is surreal for me to think that one spot on this earth can touch me with such a profound sense of tranquility. I am in awe of all of its beauty; the seagull that flies free above the water, the way the sun creates diamonds dancing upon the ocean's surface, how the sand warms my body and how the breeze cools my head. I never tire of this magical place.

Summer does enliven our senses and encourage mindfulness. We automatically feel lighter and brighter when our hearts feel joyous and grateful.

Journal about whatever comes to your mind on the days when you feel relaxed and peaceful. Allow your mind to wander to the places that bring the tranquility of spirit.

~ Threads of Reflection ~

Today I am grateful for:
Monday

_____
_____
_____
_____

Today I am grateful for:
Tuesday

_____
_____
_____
_____

Today I am grateful for:
Wednesday

_____
_____
_____
_____

Today I am grateful for: 💜
  Thursday

_____
_____
_____
_____

Today I am grateful for: 💜
  Friday

_____
_____
_____
_____

Today I am grateful for: 💜
  Saturday

_____
_____
_____
_____

Today I am grateful for: 💜
  Sunday

_____
_____
_____
_____

~Weaving Threads of Gratitude~

How do I cultivate my garden?

WEEK 28

"Words have magic. Spells and curses. Some of them, the best of them, once said, change everything."

~ Nora Roberts

*W*e may never know if our words make an impact or not, or if the timing of them is almost miraculous, but we can certainly learn how to temper them. I once assumed that someone I knew had it all; looks, brains, athleticism, so I hesitated to gush over a professional photograph of her. Suddenly I read her eyes, unsure and nervous. I recognized that she was no different than me or any of us for that matter. We all question our worth. I chose to share my admiration of her beautiful smile and hair. I watched her facial expression soften, and her eyes smile. My words were the catalyst for her happiness, and I was so pleased I had used them wisely.

We all carry within us a certain level of insecurity and uncertainty about ourselves. We continuously look for ways to relate to one another and communicate our sameness. One way we do this is through our words. Words can be gentle and nurturing with the softness of tone, or they can be cruel and sharp as the mightiest of swords. Weave your words carefully. Use them good-heartedly and without malice or cruelty. See them as an extension of your kindness and compassion. The words we carry with us and the way we convey them can make a lasting impact on our tapestry and the ones we touch.

Journal the magic of your words and how you used them to help others with kindness and love.

~ *Threads of Reflection* ~

Today I am grateful for:
  Monday

_____

_____

_____

_____

Today I am grateful for:
  Tuesday

_____

_____

_____

_____

Today I am grateful for:
  Wednesday

_____

_____

_____

_____

Today I am grateful for:
  Thursday

_____
_____
_____
_____

Today I am grateful for:
  Friday

_____
_____
_____
_____

Today I am grateful for:
  Saturday

_____
_____
_____
_____

Today I am grateful for:
  Sunday

_____
_____
_____
_____

~Weaving Threads of Gratitude~

How do I cultivate my garden?

WEEK 29

"I wear myself out and struggle with the sun. And what a sun here! It would be necessary to paint here with gold and gemstones. It is wonderful."

~ Claude Monet

I love to work in my gardens, especially my water garden. The plantings within the pond, as well as those that rim it, have unique colors and textures. But what intrigues me the most is the life within the depths of the water. I love to watch my fish swim and sun themselves in the shallows as the light streams through the magnolia tree. Every year a multitude of bullfrogs make their way to the pond and sing their croaky songs. The vintage duck decoy that bobs along the ripples of water may at times lend its back to a wayward frog who loves to go for a ride. It is in these solitary moments of my day that I become so lost in this little world that I begin to appreciate everything in my life and everyone in it.

What if we were to take notice of all the magical occurrences in our lives? We would see them as treasured gold moments. Within these instances, we would learn to value not the treasures of money and jewels, but rather the deep love and respect we have for the people that mean the most to us.

Describe how you treasure those you love. What qualities do they possess that make you want to journal about them?

~ *Threads of Reflection* ~

Today I am grateful for:
  Monday

_____
_____
_____
_____

Today I am grateful for:
  Tuesday

_____
_____
_____
_____

Today I am grateful for:
  Wednesday

_____
_____
_____
_____

Today I am grateful for:
  Thursday

_____
_____
_____
_____

Today I am grateful for:
  Friday

_____
_____
_____
_____

Today I am grateful for:
  Saturday

_____
_____
_____
_____

Today I am grateful for:
  Sunday

_____
_____
_____
_____

~Weaving Threads of Gratitude~

How do I cultivate my garden?

WEEK 30

"Soon it got dusk, a grapy dusk, a purple dusk over tangerine groves and long melon fields; the sun the color of pressed grapes, slashed with burgundy red, the fields the color of love and Spanish mysteries."

~ *Jack Kerouac*

*O*nce *when I was deep into writing my second book, I was detailing the fox that had, to me, become my spirit animal. It was dusk, and I was sitting on my patio under the twinkling lights of the gazebo that surrounded me. As I began to detail her black stocking legs, her full tail, and sweet rusty red body, I glanced up to see her sitting against a large maple tree, watching me. The sunset had fallen below the tops of the trees, spreading a spray of light across my yard. The visual of the fox within the sun was so inspiring. I realized at that moment that my writing had come to life, and I was looking upon it with awestruck eyes. An extraordinary visual set among the most beautiful sunset. This inspirational event encouraged me to experience a deeper level of mindfulness.*

Visualizing the beauty of a sultry sunset or being enveloped in the mystical calm of the night can bring about a time of self-reflection and review of the day's events. Questions left unanswered have the chance to be addressed and solved with the gift of the next sunrise.

Journal those thoughts that come to you in the quiet of the day and what profound meaning they have for you. Do they inspire you to set new goals? How will you achieve them?

~ Threads of Reflection ~

Today I am grateful for: 🩶
Monday

_____
_____
_____
_____

Today I am grateful for: 🩶
Tuesday

_____
_____
_____
_____

Today I am grateful for: 🩶
Wednesday

_____
_____
_____
_____

Today I am grateful for:
Thursday

_____
_____
_____
_____

Today I am grateful for:
Friday

_____
_____
_____
_____

Today I am grateful for:
Saturday

_____
_____
_____
_____

Today I am grateful for:
Sunday

_____
_____
_____
_____

~Weaving Threads of Gratitude~

How do I cultivate my garden?

WEEK 31

"Colors, like features, follow the changes of emotions."

~ Pablo Picasso

I have often thought the ever-changing colors of the ocean depicted its emotions. The hues from the sky can impact light from the sun and change the visual of the sea in moments. As wayward clouds float across the sun voiding its natural light, the sea would immediately switch from a happy aqua blue to mysterious emerald green in seconds. Once, when running the cliff walk in Newport at dawn on a foggy grey morning, I suddenly noticed the clouds separated over the water for just a moment. There before me, the sun slipped through the cloud cover and created a luminous tower of light beaming onto the surface of the ocean. It looked as if heaven had cast a pillar of light so bright that the surface of the water made a circumference of white. I took a picture with my phone to catch this once-in-a-lifetime moment. Clarity emerged within my being, and I suddenly felt as if I was in the presence of God.

The colors of our tapestries fluctuate with the ever-changing moments that present themselves. Although life can never be permanently smooth and steady, our wish is to keep it stable and strong. Accepting the challenges before us and moving with the flow of emotions helps us re-direct our paths forward in a positive fashion.

What positive choices did you make this week that led you onto different paths? Were there any moments that brought you clarity of purpose?

~ Threads of Reflection ~

Today I am grateful for:
   Monday

_____
_____
_____
_____

Today I am grateful for:
   Tuesday

_____
_____
_____
_____

Today I am grateful for:
   Wednesday

_____
_____
_____
_____

Today I am grateful for: ♥
  Thursday

_____
_____
_____
_____

Today I am grateful for: ♥
  Friday

_____
_____
_____
_____

Today I am grateful for: ♥
  Saturday

_____
_____
_____
_____

Today I am grateful for: ♥
  Sunday

_____
_____
_____
_____

~Weaving Threads of Gratitude~

How do I cultivate my garden?

WEEK 32

"One day, perhaps, you will see for yourself that regrets are as nothing. The value lies in how they are answered."

~ Steven Erikson

I have experienced regrets on many levels. One of my most painful regrets stemmed from my father's illness and how I handled attending his treatments. During that time, I put work before many things in my life. Once it became apparent that my father was being placed in hospice and would be leaving forever, I was able to put things in perspective and place my family obligations before my work. A sharp, poignant clarity had emerged and showed me how to correct my past regret. I remained by his side throughout hospice and was with him at his passing—a life lesson that had a profound impact on how I faced similar challenges in the future.

Regrets are part of who we are. They forge through our tapestries in some of the ugliest of colors and threads. What if we could change how we view that regret and see it as more of a learning experience or an opportunity to correct a wrong? Could we use it as a tool to re-adjust a path to avoid repeating negative experiences? Moving on and being able to see our regrets as teachable moments enhances our final picture.

Think of the pain of regret as a reminder that we are alive, capable of redirecting our efforts and weaving the life we want for ourselves. Identify past disappointments and how you have learned from them.

~ Threads of Reflection ~

Today I am grateful for:
Monday

_____
_____
_____
_____

Today I am grateful for:
Tuesday

_____
_____
_____
_____

Today I am grateful for:
Wednesday

_____
_____
_____
_____

Today I am grateful for:
  Thursday

Today I am grateful for:
  Friday

Today I am grateful for:
  Saturday

Today I am grateful for:
  Sunday

~Weaving Threads of Gratitude~

How do I cultivate my garden?

WEEK 33

"As we work to create light for others, we naturally light our own way."

~ *Mary Anne Radmacher*

I once helped an older man pay for his groceries when he was short by just a few dollars. I gave the clerk the dollar amount to cover his lack of funds and made sure he kept the change. It was so natural and straightforward, yet it had a profound effect on me. Those few moments colored my tapestry in such a way that I was inspired to continue helping others in need. It was as if in helping this total stranger, I was helping a family member or a close friend. How wonderful it is to be able to make life easier or more pleasant for others!

Even the briefest of encounters can bring about the kindest of moments. Paying it forward is an excellent way of making the world a more compassionate and gentler place. Using the gifts of time, talent, and treasure to help those around us can make a tremendous difference in not just their lives, but more distinctly, in our own.

Challenge yourself this week to simply use your smile as a way to bring forth kindness into the world. Record how a smile given to a stranger made you feel and how the stranger responded to you. Imagine the ripple effect and see where it took you.

~ Threads of Reflection ~

Today I am grateful for:
 Monday

_____
_____
_____
_____

Today I am grateful for:
 Tuesday

_____
_____
_____
_____

Today I am grateful for:
 Wednesday

_____
_____
_____
_____

Today I am grateful for:
Thursday

_____
_____
_____
_____

Today I am grateful for:
Friday

_____
_____
_____
_____

Today I am grateful for:
Saturday

_____
_____
_____
_____

Today I am grateful for:
Sunday

_____
_____
_____
_____

~Weaving Threads of Gratitude~

How do I cultivate my garden?

WEEK 34

"Throughout this journey of life we meet many people along the way. Each one has a purpose in our life. No one we meet is ever a coincidence."

~ Mimi Novac

I am a firm believer that everyone I meet along the way is there for a reason. Whether they are negative or positive interactions, all of them have an impact on my life. I have a childhood friend that instantly connected with me, and we have remained friends for over 50 years. It wasn't merely friendship, but rather a kindred spirit type of connection that tied us to one another on a spiritual level. We now see each other occasionally, but our past (our childhood in particular) has permanently tethered us together. Our treasured connection binds us with a level of love, light, and compassion that will always feel like home when we see each other.

We meet all sorts of people in our lives. Some travel on our journey for long periods, some very short, and some leave and rejoin us on a different road. Kindred spirits have a defined place in our lives and a special bond that we share. These friendships are the cornerstone of our souls. Value all of those that share that space within our being.

When journaling about the people in your life, give thought to those who have been instant and kismet. Describe the deep-seated feelings that exist between you and how it defines your relationship and why you are grateful for them.

~ *Threads of Reflection* ~

Today I am grateful for:
  Monday

_____
_____
_____
_____

Today I am grateful for:
  Tuesday

_____
_____
_____
_____

Today I am grateful for:
  Wednesday

_____
_____
_____
_____

Today I am grateful for:
  Thursday

_____
_____
_____
_____

Today I am grateful for:
  Friday

_____
_____
_____
_____

Today I am grateful for:
  Saturday

_____
_____
_____
_____

Today I am grateful for:
  Sunday

_____
_____
_____
_____

~Weaving Threads of Gratitude~

How do I cultivate my garden?

WEEK 35

"Goodbyes are only for those who love with their eyes. Because for those who love with heart and soul, there is no such thing as separation."

~ *Rumi*

*W*hen I was faced with the day I had to say my final goodbye to my beloved golden retriever, my heart felt like it would break into a million pieces. We were always inseparable, and he would often hold onto my sleeve as we walked as if to say, "I will always know where you are if I hold onto your sleeve." In his final moments, I provided a sleeve and placed it in his mouth. That gesture gave me peace and softened the hurt when the time came to say our final goodbye. In providing him that comfort, I knew he would always be near, and more importantly, he would know I would still be there for him.

Goodbyes can be filled with angst and sadness. Whether they be as simple as a trip, ending a relationship, or a final passing, we meet those moments with apprehension and dread. When envisioning that moment, we must see it with a sense of hope and love and a belief that we will all see each other again. Trust in the fact that deep love never dies—it waits beyond the veil. Express gratitude that we are blessed to know the people in our lives, and being loved by them is a gift.

When journaling about the sadness that comes with the feelings of saying goodbye, reflect on the extraordinary things that made that moment or person so special to you. Evoking memories that bring softness to the ache can be comforting and healing.

~ Threads of Reflection ~

Today I am grateful for:
   Monday

_____

Today I am grateful for:
   Tuesday

_____

Today I am grateful for:
   Wednesday

_____

Today I am grateful for:
  Thursday

_____
_____
_____
_____

Today I am grateful for:
  Friday

_____
_____
_____
_____

Today I am grateful for:
  Saturday

_____
_____
_____
_____

Today I am grateful for:
  Sunday

_____
_____
_____
_____

~Weaving Threads of Gratitude~

How do I cultivate my garden?

WEEK 36

"When it comes to life, we spin our yarn, and where we end up is really, in fact, where we always intended to be."

~ Julia Glass

I remember thinking I was a shoo-in to adopt a rescue dog I had completely fallen in love with. Finally, healing from the loss of my beloved golden retriever after 18 months, I was ready to adopt again. A male Great Pyrenees mix became available, and I knew he was perfect for my family. Unfortunately, the rescue felt he would be better suited in another home. I was crushed. I almost changed my mind entirely about adopting again, until I saw the picture of my beautiful golden retriever mix puppy – the rest is history. Not only is my girl, the sweetest and most loyal dog, but through her adoption, I was also able to form a Facebook group with all of the other puppies' owners. It has been a great experience sharing and having reunions with all the pups. I am now involved with the rescue agency, and it has fulfilled my life in a way I would never have expected.

There are times when we experience disappointment, and the feeling is beyond unbearable. We feel as though we have been cheated, somehow, from something wonderful. But what if we were to look upon that misfortune and see it differently? Many times, there are lessons to be learned from them. They can enhance the richness of our tapestries and help us grow in many different ways.

Journal about the disappointments you have faced that have ended up turning into something wonderful or brought about a positive change to your life.

~ *Threads of Reflection* ~

Today I am grateful for:
   Monday
   ♥

_____
_____
_____
_____

Today I am grateful for:
   Tuesday
   ♥

_____
_____
_____
_____

Today I am grateful for:
   Wednesday
   ♥

_____
_____
_____
_____

Today I am grateful for: ♥
   Thursday

_____
_____
_____
_____

Today I am grateful for: ♥
   Friday

_____
_____
_____
_____

Today I am grateful for: ♥
   Saturday

_____
_____
_____
_____

Today I am grateful for: ♥
   Sunday

_____
_____
_____
_____

~Weaving Threads of Gratitude~

How do I cultivate my garden?

WEEK 37

"It is by fighting the limitations, temptations, and failures
of the world that we reach our highest possibilities."

~ Helen Keller

*A*ddiction, alcoholism, depression, financial ruin, and terminal illness are all examples of afflictions that can wreak havoc in our lives. I have experienced several of those, and they all have the ability to bring you to the brink of despair. Facing them with love and support and gaining strength while overcoming these difficulties can be life-altering. Hope is the key to healing and overcoming our limitations, allowing us to be a better, more complete version of ourselves.

Hardships of all kinds require courage, hope, and support to get us through. Overcoming allows us to triumph over our afflictions and changes the course of our lives in so many positive ways. Even the smallest of hurdles can teach us a lot about ourselves. Problem-solving and finding alternative ways to better ourselves are crucial to helping us reach our highest potential.

Think of how many challenging circumstances you have faced in the past. How did you overcome those obstacles? How did you grow from this experience, and what did you learn about yourself?

~ Threads of Reflection ~

Today I am grateful for:
  Monday

_____
_____
_____
_____

Today I am grateful for:
  Tuesday

_____
_____
_____
_____

Today I am grateful for:
  Wednesday

_____
_____
_____
_____

Today I am grateful for:
  Thursday

Today I am grateful for:
  Friday

Today I am grateful for:
  Saturday

Today I am grateful for:
  Sunday

~Weaving Threads of Gratitude~

How do I cultivate my garden?

WEEK 38

"The crickets felt it was their duty to warn everybody that summertime cannot last forever. Even on the most beautiful days in the whole year – the days when summer is changing into autumn – the crickets spread the rumor of sadness and change."

~ E.B. White

*T*his particular quote carries such emotion within the words. I can actually feel the sentiment it shares. It brings to mind the time when my father was terminally ill. During that uncertain period, I embraced that summer with him, hoping to hang onto the warmth and abundance of the season and stave off the unpredictability of the months to come. As the season changed, I observed how nature had turned her leaves to vibrant yellows, reds, and oranges, silently preparing us in such a beautiful way for the end of the summer. In facing that particular autumn, I was preparing for the inevitable change within my own life. Time marks segments of our lives, and some are more poignant than others.

The changing of the seasons can be very prophetic. It means we transform into another version of ourselves, morphing with the change in weather and colors of the season. The seasons are synonymous with our life's progression. Being able to be thankful for each segment of our lives and making a point to recognize and record those moments would demonstrate how truly blessed we are.

Describe how you have grown and changed over time? Which stages had a more profound impact on your life?

~ *Threads of Reflection* ~

Today I am grateful for:
   Monday

_____
_____
_____
_____

Today I am grateful for:
   Tuesday

_____
_____
_____
_____

Today I am grateful for:
   Wednesday

_____
_____
_____
_____

Today I am grateful for:
   Thursday

_____
_____
_____
_____

Today I am grateful for:
   Friday

_____
_____
_____
_____

Today I am grateful for:
   Saturday

_____
_____
_____
_____

Today I am grateful for:
   Sunday

_____
_____
_____
_____

~Weaving Threads of Gratitude~

How do I cultivate my garden?

WEEK 39

"Thankfulness is the beginning of gratitude. Gratitude is the completion of thankfulness. Thankfulness may consist merely of words. Gratitude is shown in acts."

~ Henri Frederic Amiel

As I age, I have come to discover that a good life is celebrating ordinary moments. During my daughter's illness, just being able to do simple things like going on our annual strawberry picking day and making our bounty of jelly was a huge deal. I now see the world so differently. I embrace the simplicity of the moments that surround my family and me. I feel sincere gratitude for being able to celebrate each one of them.

If we could remind ourselves every single day to look for the incredible blessings that are around us, we would start to weave a picture that glistens and captures the miracles of those gifts. A grateful heart helps us appreciate these blessings bestowed upon us.

Journal about anything and everything that brings about your thankfulness and your gratitude. Visit this section often, for it will be a constant reminder of how valuable you are to this world.

~ Threads of Reflection ~

Today I am grateful for:
Monday

_____

_____

_____

_____

Today I am grateful for:
Tuesday

_____

_____

_____

_____

Today I am grateful for:
Wednesday

_____

_____

_____

_____

Today I am grateful for:
  Thursday

Today I am grateful for:
  Friday

Today I am grateful for:
  Saturday

Today I am grateful for:
  Sunday

~Weaving Threads of Gratitude~

How do I cultivate my garden?

WEEK 40

"Each friend represents a world in us, a world possibly not born until they arrive, and it is only by this meeting that a new world is born."

~ Anais Nin

I *have so many wonderful friends from all facets of my life, and each one represents a special gift to me. I have two friends from elementary school who are still an important part of my life. I can tell them anything without ever a fear of judgement or displeasure. Our monthly dinners and catch-up sessions are just as important and loving as the numerous sleepovers we had when we were only girls. These two incredible women are embroidered within my tapestry with the most treasured of threads: gold and silver.*

Throughout life, we experience many kinds of friendships. Whether they are life-long friends or short-term acquaintances, all of them bring vibrancy to your tapestry. Many of these relationships add color and texture to the fabric of our lives and help us become a better version of ourselves.

Journal the different ways your friends inspire you. What qualities do they possess that attracted you to them?

~ Threads of Reflection ~

Today I am grateful for: 🤍
Monday

_____
_____
_____
_____

Today I am grateful for: 🤍
Tuesday

_____
_____
_____
_____

Today I am grateful for: 🤍
Wednesday

_____
_____
_____
_____

Today I am grateful for:
  Thursday

_____
_____
_____
_____

Today I am grateful for:
  Friday

_____
_____
_____
_____

Today I am grateful for:
  Saturday

_____
_____
_____
_____

Today I am grateful for:
  Sunday

_____
_____
_____
_____

~Weaving Threads of Gratitude~

How do I cultivate my garden?

WEEK 41

"Love recognizes no barriers. It jumps hurdles, leaps fences, penetrates walls to arrive at its destination full of hope."

~ Maya Angelou

*T*here are so many levels of love, but one that stands out profoundly to me was a couple I used to greet at the doctor's office where I once worked. They were utterly devoted to each other and had a sweetness about the way they cared for one another. As the years went by, it became apparent that the woman had begun to suffer from dementia or Alzheimer's disease and had slowly begun to withdraw from the world around her. Her husband still treated her the same, conversing with her sweetly and holding her hand during the examination. To me, it was such a beautiful love. One that stood the test of time, and although the romance was no longer present, a deeper love emerged between them. I viewed their love with the most profound admiration.

The threads of love have a uniqueness to them because they are not just woven into our picture. They span, knot, and weave into so many other tapestries in our lifetime. The amount of souls we allow our hearts to welcome in only widens our tapestry. Love is the highest form of gratitude because we not only benefit by giving our affection, we glisten and shimmer with the love we receive. Our bodies may leave this earth permanently, but our love continues with those left behind.

Journal how you have received and felt profound love. How did you return that feeling?

~ *Threads of Reflection* ~

Today I am grateful for: 💜
  Monday

_____
_____
_____
_____

Today I am grateful for: 💜
  Tuesday

_____
_____
_____
_____

Today I am grateful for: 💜
  Wednesday

_____
_____
_____
_____

Today I am grateful for:
  Thursday

_____
_____
_____
_____

Today I am grateful for:
  Friday

_____
_____
_____
_____

Today I am grateful for:
  Saturday

_____
_____
_____
_____

Today I am grateful for:
  Sunday

_____
_____
_____
_____

~Weaving Threads of Gratitude~

How do I cultivate my garden?

WEEK 42

"Sometimes, reaching out and taking someone's hand is the beginning of a journey. At other times, it is allowing another to take yours."

~ *Vera Nazarian*

*W*hen I think about putting myself out there, I am overwhelmed with an abundance of emotions. Fear of rejection or regret takes over my impulse. But one time, in particular, I reached out to an old high school friend I had not seen or spoken to in years. She had placed a single pink heart on her Facebook page with the name St. Jude. Oddly, I had prayed that morning to St. Jude, asking for a blessing for my ailing father. Reaching out to her, I learned that she, too, was praying for her sick father. Together, we walked a road of support, grief, and remembrance. That gesture made a permanent impact on the quality of that journey and renewed our friendship.

Cast your threads out with the belief that what you put out will potentially come back to you in the future. Courage, strength, and faith are required when putting yourself out there. That process can be scary and unsure. But what if we kept ourselves open to the idea that every cast sent forth might be life-changing! Not all will come back with a positive return, but the ones that do could make all the difference in the weaving of our life's picture.

Can you think of a time when you reached out to someone and formed an impactful connection? What were the circumstances that compelled you to connect with that person?

~ Threads of Reflection ~

Today I am grateful for:
  Monday

_____
_____
_____
_____

Today I am grateful for:
  Tuesday

_____
_____
_____
_____

Today I am grateful for:
  Wednesday

_____
_____
_____
_____

Today I am grateful for:
  Thursday

_____
_____
_____
_____

Today I am grateful for:
  Friday

_____
_____
_____
_____

Today I am grateful for:
  Saturday

_____
_____
_____
_____

Today I am grateful for:
  Sunday

_____
_____
_____
_____

~Weaving Threads of Gratitude~

How do I cultivate my garden?

WEEK 43

"If wrinkles must be written upon our brows, let them not be written upon the heart. The spirit should never grow old."

~ James A. Garfield

*T*hrough many years of vacationing at my favorite beach in Newport, Rhode Island, I would observe two older women who frequented the beach at the same time each day. These two women would don the same white bathing caps and tether Styrofoam boogie boards to their wrists as they would enter the water's edge. Then, like synchronized swimmers, they waded, dunked, and swam at the same time.

Once, in the water, they would ride the waves over and over for about 45 minutes, their old bodies taking on a youthful appearance as they would laugh and play in the surf. Then, just like clockwork, they would stop and slowly return to their beach blanket on the shore, resuming the age of their bodies, not of their minds. I marveled at their quest for youthful play and made a note of the gift of childlike qualities.

Possessing this gift allows us to keep our tapestries vibrant and our souls playful. There are many ways to enhance our inner child. Participate in those moments that make your heart feel young, and you will blossom with the joy of seeing the world with new eyes again.

Journal the activities and moments of your life that bring about the fountain of youth vibe to your soul. Practice those moments often.

~ Threads of Reflection ~

Today I am grateful for:
  Monday

_____
_____
_____
_____

Today I am grateful for:
  Tuesday

_____
_____
_____
_____

Today I am grateful for:
  Wednesday

_____
_____
_____
_____

Today I am grateful for:
  Thursday

_____
_____
_____
_____

Today I am grateful for:
  Friday

_____
_____
_____
_____

Today I am grateful for:
  Saturday

_____
_____
_____
_____

Today I am grateful for:
  Sunday

_____
_____
_____
_____

~Weaving Threads of Gratitude~

How do I cultivate my garden?

WEEK 44

"Time flies over us but leaves its shadow behind."

~ Nathaniel Hawthorne

I find that meditating by my koi pond is an excellent way to embrace time. There, watching and listening to nature, my breathing is slower, my mind clearer, and my thoughts become positive. Spending time in my special place, I can recall parts of my day that made me smile. Those memories create a thankfulness within me. Negative thoughts that creep into my mind are redirected so that I can find something pleasant about them. Time cannot stand still, but improving the quality of my quiet moments creates gratefulness within me.

Our time on this planet is short, and giving value to our present, cherishing our past, and embracing what is yet to be is how we bring clarity to our life. Examining the parts of our day in the quietude of a unique space, we begin to see more clearly how time passes, but the moments remain vibrant and colorful.

Is there a place where you feel most inspired—a space where you feel a sense of purpose, clarity, and wisdom to look at your life with unconditional love. Does the quality of time you spend there encourage peace and tranquility?

~ Threads of Reflection ~

Today I am grateful for:
Monday

_____

_____

_____

_____

Today I am grateful for:
Tuesday

_____

_____

_____

_____

Today I am grateful for:
Wednesday

_____

_____

_____

_____

Today I am grateful for: 💜
  Thursday

_____
_____
_____
_____

Today I am grateful for: 💜
  Friday

_____
_____
_____
_____

Today I am grateful for: 💜
  Saturday

_____
_____
_____
_____

Today I am grateful for: 💜
  Sunday

_____
_____
_____
_____

~Weaving Threads of Gratitude~

How do I cultivate my garden?

WEEK 45

"We don't accomplish anything in this world alone... and whatever happens is the result of the whole tapestry of one's life and all the weavings of individual threads form one to another that creates something."

~ Sandra Day O'Connor

*H*ave you ever thought about the places and the people who have inspired you? I once made a trek up to the Berkshires into Stockbridge, Massachusetts, to visit the Shrine of the Divine Mercies. I had a dream of an angel sitting on the side of a mountain looking down upon me as I hiked up a windy gravel path. That dream brought about my finding the Shrine of the Divine Mercies and walking its grounds. There among the tops of the great pines and the beautiful statues, I found a peace I had not sensed for quite some time. I will never forget how close to God I felt that day. When these sacred places arise before us, it can be life-changing. They call to our spiritual essence and fashion the weavings that help create our grand masterpiece.

Using your threads for positive enlightenment is what will enhance your life and your grand picture. Follow these paths with good intentions and kindness, keep expanding your world in beautiful ways, and continue to embrace new connections that will keep your tapestry strong and resilient.

Describe within this journal what made you feel a greater connection to your higher power. How do you see your tapestry and the glorious threads that compose it?

~ *Threads of Reflection* ~

Today I am grateful for:
  Monday

_____
_____
_____
_____

Today I am grateful for:
  Tuesday

_____
_____
_____
_____

Today I am grateful for:
  Wednesday

_____
_____
_____
_____

Today I am grateful for:
  Thursday

_____
_____
_____
_____

Today I am grateful for:
  Friday

_____
_____
_____
_____

Today I am grateful for:
  Saturday

_____
_____
_____
_____

Today I am grateful for:
  Sunday

_____
_____
_____
_____

~Weaving Threads of Gratitude~

How do I cultivate my garden?

WEEK 46

"White is our blank page, our openness to what is to be, and reflects the light of our transition into the next world: heaven."

~ Judith Cosby

*A*s I held my father's hand in his last moments before he passed, I opened a window in a gesture of spiritual freeness. My Dad had been in hospice for six days after waging a battle with colon cancer. At the moment I opened that window, the sun streamed in with bright light. Outside the window, beyond my parents' backyard, was the border of woods to a state park. Standing along the edge were several deer looking at the room from a distance. The stag stood stoic and strong. Seconds later and with no apparent reason, they ran along the forest edge and back into the dense thicket, and I was struck by the beauty of the moment. I felt as though the deer came to pay homage, and as they ran, my father was there to usher them along.

When we see our life with newness and spiritual awakening, we become acutely aware of how wonderous we genuinely are and how profoundly important we are to this world. Signs may present themselves, and if we are open to seeing them, they add depth and beauty to the occasion.

What experiences have you had that have heightened your spiritual awareness? Do you have specific objects that elicit ethereal connotations such as feathers, butterflies, dragonflies, heart rocks, or other reminders of these connections in your life?

~ *Threads of Reflection* ~

Today I am grateful for:
  Monday

_____
_____
_____
_____

Today I am grateful for:
  Tuesday

_____
_____
_____
_____

Today I am grateful for:
  Wednesday

_____
_____
_____
_____

Today I am grateful for: ♥
  Thursday

Today I am grateful for: ♥
  Friday

Today I am grateful for: ♥
  Saturday

Today I am grateful for: ♥
  Sunday

~Weaving Threads of Gratitude~

How do I cultivate my garden?

WEEK 47

"I meet people, and they become chapters in my stories."

~ Avijeet Das

*M*eeting new people in my life has been such an enjoyable experience. I tend to view every new soul as a chance to better myself. Since I have become an author, I have been invited to attend several book clubs that selected my memoir, Threads, as their reading selection. It has been an incredible experience hearing the readers share their own experiences and struggles and how they related them to the chapters in Threads. Every chance I get, I drink in their stories and witness the incredible challenges they have overcome, the amazing feats they have conquered, and the wondrous places they have visited.

New friendships and acquaintances also enrich our tapestries. Being open to the differences of others and the knowledge and views they bring to our lives can help us grow. All forms of new souls have a purpose in life. Positive encounters can bring forth a colorful and dynamic vibe to all those we meet. Negative encounters, although unpleasant and at times damaging, can re-direct our lives onto another path. Regardless of how we greet the new souls in our lives, each one is a miracle. Each one can influence our world.

How many new people did you meet this week that made an impact on you? What significant ways did their connection touch you?

~ Threads of Reflection ~

Today I am grateful for: 🩶
   Monday

_____
_____
_____
_____

Today I am grateful for: 🩶
   Tuesday

_____
_____
_____
_____

Today I am grateful for: 🩶
   Wednesday

_____
_____
_____
_____

Today I am grateful for:
  Thursday

_____

_____

_____

_____

Today I am grateful for:
  Friday

_____

_____

_____

_____

Today I am grateful for:
  Saturday

_____

_____

_____

_____

Today I am grateful for:
  Sunday

_____

_____

_____

_____

~Weaving Threads of Gratitude~

How do I cultivate my garden?

WEEK 48

The purpose of life is to live it, to taste experience to the utmost, to reach out eagerly and without fear for newer and richer experience."

~ Eleanor Roosevelt

I had always wanted to be a triathlete but felt I lacked the excellent physical shape to participate in a triathlon. A friend was training for a sprint triathlon to support breast cancer and asked if I was interested. This race was my chance, and it helped a worthy cause! I entered the competition and trained hard in all categories; swimming, biking, and running. The day finally came, and I finished my first triathlon! It was arduous but so rewarding to hear my name called out as I ran over the finish line. That first triathlon was significant to my life. It encouraged me to continue this adventure and ultimately taught me to improve my performance with each race. I was able to compete in a total of four triathlons before retiring and switching my goal to running in road races.

Embracing new experiences can instill a mixture of emotions, often met with the exhilaration of excitement, and a level of trepidation all rolled into one. We must experience new things for our tapestry to continue to grow to its fullest potential. The enrichment of these moments and the connections we make in doing so have a profound impact on who we can become.

What ideas or goals would you put into a bucket list of endless possibilities? Do you envision a timeframe to make even a few happen? Journal your thoughts and why you desire to meet those goals?

~ *Threads of Reflection* ~

Today I am grateful for:
   Monday

_____
_____
_____
_____

Today I am grateful for:
   Tuesday

_____
_____
_____
_____

Today I am grateful for:
   Wednesday

_____
_____
_____
_____

Today I am grateful for:
  Thursday

_____

Today I am grateful for:
  Friday

_____

Today I am grateful for:
  Saturday

_____

Today I am grateful for:
  Sunday

_____

~Weaving Threads of Gratitude~

How do I cultivate my garden?

WEEK 49

"We look at life from the backside of the tapestry. And most of the time, what we see is the loose threads, tangled knots, and the like. But occasionally, God's light shines through the tapestry, and we get a glimpse of the larger design with God weaving together the darks and lights of existence."

~ John Piper

*B*eing able to obtain a deeper glimpse into your life and visualize the bigger picture is a gift. While going through a challenging year with the health of my youngest daughter, I became acutely aware of the profound magnitude of what had occurred during that time. Upon deep self-reflection, I witnessed how intense my faith had become. An acceptance emerged into my being and allowed me to see the grand picture. From the start of that tumultuous year, until the end of it, nothing had changed health-wise, but what had changed was my acceptance, courage, and faith. When the larger design emerged, and I looked beyond the tangled mess of threads, what I saw was trust in my higher power and conviction in my soul.

We can, at times, get lost within the rut of life and miss many of the amazing things around us. Embracing God and allowing his love to touch us, we begin to see the bigger picture. We are but a small and beautiful part of the grand design, and in recognizing that, we know the importance of our worth.

Journal how you see your higher power's light shining into your tapestry. Where do you see the inspiration in your life?

~ *Threads of Reflection* ~

Today I am grateful for:
   Monday

_____
_____
_____
_____

Today I am grateful for:
   Tuesday

_____
_____
_____
_____

Today I am grateful for:
   Wednesday

_____
_____
_____
_____

Today I am grateful for:
  Thursday

_____
_____
_____
_____

Today I am grateful for:
  Friday

_____
_____
_____
_____

Today I am grateful for:
  Saturday

_____
_____
_____
_____

Today I am grateful for:
  Sunday

_____
_____
_____
_____

~Weaving Threads of Gratitude~

How do I cultivate my garden?

WEEK 50

"White is not a mere absence of color; it is a shining and affirmative thing, as fierce as red, as definite as black. God paints in many colors; but He never paints so gorgeously, I had almost said so gaudily, as when He paints in white."

~ G.K. Chesterton

*A*nother quote I absolutely love! It reminds me of how my spirituality has grown in so many directions. I feel close to God by the ocean, in the woods, in my garden, and at my church. In those places, I feel entirely connected to my higher power. There is a sense of harmony within those spaces that nourishes my thoughts. Trusting the Divine means trusting myself and allowing a positive balance in my life. Although I delight in the entire spectrum of colors, it is the purity of white that remains a sacred color for me and brings my faithful heart to bear.

Our spiritual journey leads us to the places where we feel divinely connected. Our willingness to find these areas is essential to deepening our spirituality. Those activities that quiet the mind and encourage reflective thought bring us closer to our higher power.

Journal about the ways you have experienced spiritual awakenings. How has your faith grown over time? Are there specific places or people who have encouraged that growth?

~*Threads of Reflection*~

Today I am grateful for:
  Monday

_____
_____
_____
_____

Today I am grateful for:
  Tuesday

_____
_____
_____
_____

Today I am grateful for:
  Wednesday

_____
_____
_____
_____

Today I am grateful for: 💜
   Thursday

_____
_____
_____
_____

Today I am grateful for: 💜
   Friday

_____
_____
_____
_____

Today I am grateful for: 💜
   Saturday

_____
_____
_____
_____

Today I am grateful for: 💜
   Sunday

_____
_____
_____
_____

~Weaving Threads of Gratitude~

How do I cultivate my garden?

WEEK 51

"There's a treasure hidden in every moment. The joy of life is finding it."

~ Katrina Mayer

I enjoy the simplicity of sitting out on my beloved patio and embracing the quietness of the area. I have decorated the gazebo with twinkling lights and cozy furniture and have surrounded it with an abundance of beautiful flowers and plants. Each moment spent out there becomes a treasure of time encapsulated in the warmth of summer. Friends and family gather there and treat it as a mecca of peace and love, sharing their gift of time with me.

Some of the most incredible things that we experience appear minuscule, but upon review or reflection, shine with more significant meaning. Hindsight can be very revealing and prompt us to see things with a clearer vision. Appreciation for even the smallest of miracles can bring forth such deep feelings of gratitude and awe. Never take for granted the little things in life, but rather see the multi-faceted moments that surround you daily and journal the ones that warm the heart.

Think about the time spent with the people you love most. When you recall those relationships and the occasions spent together, were you able to recognize the importance of the moments? Journal the ways hindsight helped bring clarity and thankfulness for those encounters.

~ *Threads of Reflection* ~

Today I am grateful for:
  Monday

_____

_____

_____

_____

Today I am grateful for:
  Tuesday

_____

_____

_____

_____

Today I am grateful for:
  Wednesday

_____

_____

_____

_____

Today I am grateful for:
  Thursday

Today I am grateful for:
  Friday

Today I am grateful for:
  Saturday

Today I am grateful for:
  Sunday

~Weaving Threads of Gratitude~

How do I cultivate my garden?

WEEK 52

"Sunrise paints the sky with pinks and the sunset with peaches. Cool to warm. So is the progression from childhood to old age."

~ Vera Nazarian

*A*s a child, I played and trusted with innocent and fresh eyes. Then I began my teenage years, filled with hopes and dreams, romances, and career choices. As I entered into adulthood, I bought a home, married my college sweetheart, bore two children, and continued my career. As I progress now into my later years, my views have softened, my desires are simple, and I quietly prepare for my last phase. I concentrate on manifesting good things—things that bring peace of heart.

Sunrises and sunsets not only mark the progression of time but the accomplishments of our day. We are reborn every dawn with the hopes and aspirations of the moments to come, and we rest each evening with the gratefulness of what we were able to achieve. This visual is how we inscribe our gratefulness, no matter how small or large, within our hearts and acknowledge its gifts.

How do you acknowledge your gratefulness daily? How do you demonstrate it to others? What are you most grateful for as you review your life in its entirety?

~ Threads of Reflection ~

Today I am grateful for:
  Monday

_____

_____

_____

_____

Today I am grateful for:
  Tuesday

_____

_____

_____

_____

Today I am grateful for:
  Wednesday

_____

_____

_____

_____

Today I am grateful for:
  Thursday

_____
_____
_____
_____

Today I am grateful for:
  Friday

_____
_____
_____
_____

Today I am grateful for:
  Saturday

_____
_____
_____
_____

Today I am grateful for:
  Sunday

_____
_____
_____
_____

~Weaving Threads of Gratitude~

How do I cultivate my garden?

"Life requires work, planning, and progression to keep in step with future growth. But it is the appreciation of time that makes our life invaluable. In doing so, time is temporarily halted, captured in the moments colored by the beauty and love that surrounds us.

Take the time to enjoy the view. Don't sweat the small stuff. Focus on what's important in life and try not to let time dictate the pace of the journey."

~Judith Cosby

A Message from the Author

Thank you for purchasing Weaving Threads of Gratitude. If you enjoyed this journal, please consider leaving a review at the following websites:

www.amazon.com

and

www.barnesandnoble.com

For more information, please visit me at the following:

https://www.judithcosby.com

https://www.facebook.com/JudithAnnCosby

https://www.linkedin.com/in/judith-cosby-799079124

https://www.instagram.com/judy.r.cosby

https://twitter.com/cosby_judith

judithacosby@gmail.com

Also, by Judith Cosby

Threads

A journey into the picture of the soul

&

Spirit Threads

Messages of hope and healing